# my first Cookbook

Written by Elizabeth Sewell
Illustrated by Jan Howarth

PRINTED IN
DEAN &
41/43 Ludgate Hill
TRADE MARK
GREAT BRITAIN
SON Ltd.
LONDON EC4

# Contents

Edited by Helen Frazer/Designed by Dominique Clarke
© Copyright Paul Hamlyn Pty Limited 1973
This edition published by DEAN & SON, LTD. 1975
603 06002 1

# Introduction

Here is a cookbook just for you!

Cooking is great fun and the results are delicious. The recipes in this book have been specially chosen for you because they are easy to follow. Cooking is a wonderful hobby for girls and boys alike. With just the everyday cooking equipment your mother uses, you can start practising straight away. Ask her to help you at first and very soon you will find you are able to 'whip up' dishes for your family and friends. You'll really be popular then!

Ask your mother if you can go shopping with her, and help select the ingredients for the dishes you are going to make. Choose ingredients carefully and make sure that meat, vegetables and fruit are fresh.

In this book we have included dishes suitable for everyday meals—Baked Cheese Eggs, Chicken Cacciatora, Italian Spaghetti, Tossed Green Salad and Pineapple Upside-Down Cake. There are also recipes for quick snacks and party foods—Egg Men, Frankfurter and Pineapple Kebabs, Banana Delight and Pineapple Boat. All the dishes are delicious and ideal for serving on special occasions.

There's no dull food here, and all the recipes teach you the things you must know about cooking and include the basic cooking methods. When you have mastered these, you will be able to cook dishes from other cookbooks. And it won't be too long before you will be able to make up your own variations to recipes.

Now read the recipes and follow the instructions carefully. Then you will always be welcome to try your hand in the kitchen. Your family and friends will love trying your dishes too—but don't forget to leave enough for yourself!

*Elizabeth Sewell*

# Hints to Guide You

- Always wear an apron, comfortable shoes, and working clothes.
- Before you start work, carefully read the recipe and be sure that you understand the instructions.
- Collect your equipment and weigh the ingredients **before** you start to cook.
- Close-at-hand, have a bowl for all scraps and a dishcloth or sponge for wiping down the bench.
- Follow the pictures exactly. They will show you how to do each step correctly.
- Wash your cooking equipment as you go along so that you can use it again.
- If you spill anything on the stove, clean it up immediately while it is easy to remove...but be careful not to burn your fingers.
- Thoroughly rinse all unpeeled fruit and vegetables to remove germs, insecticides and other poisonous substances that may have been sprayed on to them.
- Be careful when using sharp knives. (Ask your mother to show you how to use them correctly.)
- Chop all fruit, vegetables and meats on a chopping board.
- To core fruit, use a knife or an apple corer.
- If your mother does not have a garlic crusher, peel the garlic, chop it on a board, cover with ½ teaspoon salt, and squash together with the blade of a knife until it forms a paste.
- The simplest way to break an egg is to tap it gently on the side of a bowl, and when cracked, pull the eggshell apart and let the egg drop into the bowl.
- Grate cheese from a large piece held firmly between the fingertips to avoid scraping your knuckles on the sharp grates.
- To place long spaghetti in a saucepan of water without breaking it: bring the water to a rapid boil; then, holding the spaghetti at one end, gently lower it into the water. (As it enters the water, the spaghetti will soften and curve around the pan.)
- Always use an oven cloth or oven mitts when removing hot dishes from the oven or a hot-plate.
- Choose your cooking oil from olive, safflower, peanut or any other commercial variety available at the supermarket.
- Never put any prepared foods into the oven until it is heated to the required temperature.
- When baking, don't open the oven door to check on the food until the specified time is up. If you do, cooler air will get into the oven and reduce the heat, which could spoil the dish you are cooking.

- A good cook always tastes for seasoning. Use a teaspoon and be careful not to burn yourself.
- To test if a cake is cooked: 1. Touch the top lightly with your finger. If cooked, the cake will spring back in shape. 2. Insert a clean skewer in the middle of the cake. If the cake is cooked, the skewer will still be clean when removed.
  It is helpful to remember that a cooked cake shrinks slightly around the edges.
- Remove a cake from a cake tin by letting the cake cool in the tin for a few minutes, then sliding a round bladed knife around the inner edge of the tin to loosen the cake from it, and turning the cake on to a wire cooling tray.
- To roll pastry, place the dough on a lightly floured board. Lightly flour a rolling pin and roll pastry gently, but firmly, using even pressure, until it is the required thickness. While rolling, turn the dough regularly to make sure that it does not stick to the board. If necessary, sprinkle the board and rolling pin with more flour.
- Always leave the kitchen clean and tidy. And after all that hard work, don't forget about the food you're cooking!

# Weights and Measures

In this cookbook, we give you both metric and imperial measures—FOLLOW ONLY ONE COLUMN.
When using metric measures, you will need a standard metric measuring cup (250 millilitres capacity). You will also need a set of Australian standard measuring spoons. The Australian standard tablespoon has a capacity of 20 millilitres and the Australian standard teaspoon has a capacity of 5 millilitres.
When using imperial measures, you will need a standard imperial measuring cup (8 fluid ounces capacity) and a set of Australian standard measuring spoons. Like the metric measure spoons, the Australian standard tablespoon has a capacity of 20 millilitres and the Australian standard teaspoon has a capacity of 5 millilitres.
All measurements listed are level. To obtain a level spoon measure, fill the spoon, hold it steady, and scrape the flat edge of a knife across the top of the spoon.
A pinch is the amount you can hold between your thumb and forefinger.
The British imperial pint (used in Australia) has a volume of 20 fluid ounces.
All fats are given in grams and ounces. A new packet can be marked off in weight portions.
All vegetables and meats are given in grams and kilograms, and ounces and pounds, because they can be bought in these quantities.

ABBREVIATIONS:

| | |
|---|---|
| gram: g | ounce: oz |
| millilitre: ml | pound: lb |
| | fluid ounce: fl oz |

# Cookery Terms

**Bake:** To cook in dry heat in an oven. (Without fats, oils or liquids.)

**Bind:** To combine ingredients together completely.

**Blend:** To mix ingredients together until combined.

**Boil:** A mixture is boiling when bubbles rise rapidly to the surface.

**Core, to:** To remove cores from fruit.

**Cream, to:** To blend a fat with other ingredients until light and fluffy.

**Decorate:** To improve the appearance and flavour of a sweet dish by adding whipped cream, glacé cherries, nuts, etc.

**Flameproof Dish:** A dish that can be placed on a hot-plate as well as in the oven.

**Fry:** To cook in hot fat or oil.

**Garnish, to:** To improve the appearance and flavour of a savoury dish by adding chopped parsley, grated cheese, etc.

**Grease, to:** To rub the surface of a bowl, cake tin or baking tray with a buttered paper, or to 'paint' the surface with a lightly oiled pastry brush.

**Grill:** A quick method of cooking by radiant heat. (The food is placed close to a pre-heated griller.)

**Hull, to:** To remove small green leaves and stalks from strawberries and other berry fruits.

**Knead:** To work dough with your hands until it is smooth. (Ask your mother to show you how to do this correctly.)

**Ovenproof Dish:** A dish that can be placed in the oven but *not* on a hot-plate.

**Roll, to:** To flatten dough to a required thickness with a rolling pin.

**Season, to:** To improve the flavour of food by adding salt, pepper, other spices, and/or herbs.

**Shell, to:** To remove outer coating from foods such as peas and hard-boiled eggs.

**Shred, to:** To slice finely with a sharp knife.

**Sieve, to:** To remove lumps from a food such as flour or sugar by putting it through a sieve.

**Simmer:** A mixture is simmering when only an occasional bubble shows on the surface.

**Toast, to:** To brown food under a hot griller or in a toaster.

**Whisk, to:** To mix with a rotary beater or hand whisk.

# Green Salad

SERVES: 4-6

# ingredients

lettuce
small cucumber
celery
shallots
green capsicum
commercial mayonnaise or French dressing

# metric and imperial

1
1
2 stalks
4
1
to serve

# equipment

chopping board
vegetable knife
vegetable peeler
plastic bag
glass or wooden salad bowl

# method

1 Wash vegetables thoroughly under running cold water. Drain.

2 Tear lettuce into bite-sized pieces.

3 Peel cucumber and slice thinly.

4 Slice celery and shallots, discarding any discoloured outer pieces.

5 Remove seeds from capsicum and slice thinly.

6 Place all ingredients in a plastic bag and chill in refrigerator until ready to serve.

7 Arrange green salad in a large wooden or glass salad bowl.

8 Serve with a jug of mayonnaise or French dressing.

# Garlic Bread

SERVES: 4

## ingredients

| | metric | imperial |
|---|---|---|
| butter or margarine | 185 g | 6 oz |
| dried mixed herbs | 1 teaspoon | 1 teaspoon |
| lemon juice | 1 teaspoon | 1 teaspoon |
| ground black pepper | pinch | pinch |
| garlic, crushed | 2 cloves | 2 cloves |
| French bread | 1 loaf | 1 loaf |

## equipment

teaspoon measure
lemon squeezer
garlic crusher
mixing bowl
mixing spoon

bread board
bread knife
round-bladed knife
aluminium foil
bread basket or serving dish

# method

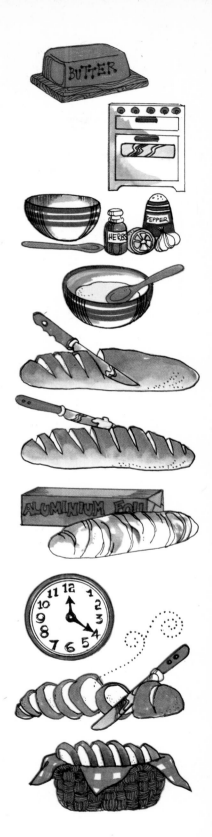

1 Take butter out of refrigerator in advance, to soften.

2 Set oven temperature at 200-230°C (400-450°F).

3 Place butter in a mixing bowl with herbs, lemon juice, pepper and crushed garlic.

4 With a mixing spoon, beat together thoroughly until creamed.

5 Cut the loaf in even, slanting slices, about 2 cm (¾ inch) thick, without cutting through the lower crust.

6 Spread each slice with creamed butter.

7 Reshape the loaf and securely wrap in aluminium foil.

8 Place in a hot oven for 20 minutes until bread is hot and golden.

9 Unwrap and cut through lower crust of bread.

10 Serve warm in a bread basket or serving dish.

# SweetCorn Soup

SERVES: 4

## ingredients

| ingredients | metric | imperial |
|---|---|---|
| sweet corn | 315 g can | 10 oz can |
| water | 935 ml | 3¾ cups |
| chicken stock cubes | 2 | 2 |
| butter or margarine | 60 g | 2 oz |
| plain flour | 4 tablespoons | 4 tablespoons |
| milk | 500 ml | 2 cups |
| salt | ¼ teaspoon | ¼ teaspoon |
| ground pepper | pinch | pinch |
| hot buttered toast | to serve | to serve |

## equipment

can opener
cup measure
tablespoon measure
¼ teaspoon measure

large saucepan
medium saucepan
mixing spoon
soup bowls or mugs

# method

1   Place the sweet corn, water and chicken stock cubes in a large saucepan.

2   Simmer gently for 20 minutes.

3   In a medium saucepan, melt butter over a moderate heat.

4   Add flour and stir until smooth. Cook for 1-2 minutes.

5   Add milk and, stirring continuously, cook until sauce is thickened and smooth. Remove from heat.

6   Pour white sauce into sweet corn mixture and stir well.

7   Add salt and pepper. Reheat soup.

8   Serve in soup bowls or mugs with hot buttered toast.

# Egg Men
**SERVES: 4**

# ingredients

eggs
pickled onions
capers
stuffed olives
parsley sprigs
lettuce leaves

# metric and imperic

4
4
8
2
4
to serve

# equipment

saucepan
spoon
sharp knife
cocktail sticks
serving plate

# method

1 Using a spoon, carefully place the eggs in a saucepan of boiling water and boil for 10 minutes.

2 Place saucepan containing hard-boiled eggs under cold running water. When water in saucepan is cool, crack eggs and leave in water for at least five minutes.

3 Shell hard-boiled eggs.

4 Cut a thin slice off the blunt end of each egg and reserve.

5 With a cocktail stick, secure pickled onion to pointed end of each egg for a head. Top with egg slice for a hat.

6 Using pieces of a cocktail stick, place 2 capers on to onion for eyes.

7 Place a slice of stuffed olive on egg for a button.

8 Tuck a sprig of parsley into neck for a scarf.

9 Wash lettuce leaves thoroughly. Shred finely with a knife.

10 Place shredded lettuce on a serving plate and place Egg Men on top.

# Baked Cheese Eggs

SERVES: 4

| ingredients | metric | imperial |
|---|---|---|
| cheddar cheese | 125 g | 4 oz |
| eggs | 4 | 4 |
| salt and pepper | to season | to season |
| fresh cream | 4 tablespoons | 4 tablespoons |
| fingers of hot buttered toast | to serve | to serve |

## equipment

4 ovenproof ramekins
baking tray
grater
tablespoon measure

# method

1 Set oven temperature at 170-190°C (350-375°F).

2 Grease 4 small ovenproof ramekins with butter and place on a baking tray.

3 Grate cheese.

4 Sprinkle half the cheese into the ramekins.

5 Carefully break 1 egg into each ramekin.

6 Season with salt and pepper.

7 Pour a spoonful of cream on top of each egg.

8 Sprinkle with remaining cheese.

9 Bake eggs in a moderate oven for 15 minutes, until set.

10 Serve with fingers of hot buttered toast.

# Frankfurter and Pineapple Kebab

SERVES: 4

## ingredients

| ingredients | metric | imperial |
|---|---|---|
| frankfurters | 4 | 4 |
| pineapple pieces | 470 g can | 15 oz can |
| butter or margarine | 30 g | 1 oz |

## equipment

can opener
4 metal skewers
chopping board
knife
small saucepan
pastry brush

# method

1    Cut each frankfurter into 4 pieces.

2    Drain pineapple pieces.

3    Put pieces of frankfurter and pineapple alternately on 4 metal skewers, to make kebabs.

4    Pre-heat griller.

5    Place kebabs in grill pan. (Remove grid from pan.)

6    Melt butter and brush over kebabs.

7    Place under grill for 5 minutes.

8    Turn kebabs over, brush again with melted butter, and grill on other side for 5 minutes.

9    Serve hot on skewers.

# Scalloped Potatoes

SERVES: 4

## ingredients

| ingredients | metric | imperial |
|---|---|---|
| garlic, crushed | 1 clove | 1 clove |
| potatoes | 500 g | 1 lb |
| salt | 1 teaspoon | 1 teaspoon |
| ground pepper | ¼ teaspoon | ¼ teaspoon |
| milk | 125 ml | ½ cup |
| grated Swiss cheese | 125 ml | ½ cup |
| butter or margarine | 30 g | 1 oz |
| chopped parsley | to garnish | to garnish |

## equipment

teaspoon measure
¼ teaspoon measure
cup measure
garlic crusher
potato peeler

chopping board
vegetable knife
grater
ovenproof casserole
small saucepan

# method

1. Set oven temperature at 170-190°C (350-375°F).

2. Grease an ovenproof casserole.

3. Spread garlic over base of casserole.

4. Scrub, peel and thinly slice potatoes.

5. Place sliced potato in layers in prepared casserole, seasoning each layer with salt and pepper.

6. Bring milk to boiling point (watch carefully) in a small saucepan and pour over potatoes in casserole.

7. Sprinkle cheese on top and dot with small pieces of butter.

8. Cook in a moderate oven for 30-45 minutes until potatoes are tender and brown on top.

9. Serve garnished with chopped parsley.

# Baked Bean Hot Pot

SERVES: 4

## ingredients

| ingredients | metric | imperial |
|---|---|---|
| frankfurters | 8 | 8 |
| large onion | 1 | 1 |
| green capsicum | 1 | 1 |
| butter or margarine | 30 g | 1 oz |
| baked beans in tomato sauce | 500 g can | 16 oz can |

## equipment

chopping board
vegetable knife
medium saucepan
mixing spoon
can opener

# method

1   Cut frankfurters into 5 cm (2 inch) lengths.

2   Peel and slice onion.

3   Remove seeds from capsicum and chop finely.

4   Melt butter in a saucepan over a moderate heat and cook onion and capsicum until tender, stirring occasionally.

5   Add baked beans and frankfurters.

6   Cover saucepan, reduce heat to low, and cook hot-pot for 15 minutes.

7   Serve in bowls. (For a special occasion, this meal is delicious eaten with rashers of crisply fried bacon.)

# Italian Spaghetti

SERVES: 4

# ingredients

| ingredients | metric | imperial |
|---|---|---|
| green capsicum | 1 | 1 |
| onions | 2 | 2 |
| cooking oil | 2 tablespoons | 2 tablespoons |
| garlic, crushed | 1 clove | 1 clove |
| minced steak | 500 g | 1 lb |
| peeled tomatoes | 440 g can | 14 oz can |
| Worcestershire sauce | 1 tablespoon | 1 tablespoon |
| salt | 1 teaspoon | 1 teaspoon |
| ground pepper | pinch | pinch |
| spaghetti | 375 g packet | 12 oz packet |
| grated Parmesan cheese | to serve | to serve |

# equipment

tablespoon measure
teaspoon measure
garlic crusher (optional)
can opener
chopping board
vegetable knife

medium saucepan
mixing spoon
large saucepan
colander
serving dish

28

# method

1. Remove seeds from capsicum and chop finely.

2. Peel and slice onions.

3. Heat oil in a medium saucepan over a moderate heat and add capsicum, garlic and onion. Cook, stirring occasionally, until onion is golden brown.

4. Add minced steak and continue to cook, stirring occasionally, until meat turns brown.

5. Add tomatoes, Worcestershire sauce, salt and pepper. Stir well.

6. Reduce heat to low, cover saucepan, and cook spaghetti sauce for 20 minutes.

7. Bring a large saucepan of water to the boil. Add spaghetti and stir well.

8. Simmer, uncovered, over a moderate heat for approximately 15 minutes, until spaghetti is tender.

9. Drain spaghetti in a colander.

10. To serve, place spaghetti in a serving dish, spoon meat sauce over, and sprinkle with Parmesan cheese.

# Chicken Cacciatora

SERVES: 4

# ingredients

| ingredients | metric | imperial |
|---|---|---|
| onions | 2 | 2 |
| cooking oil | 4 tablespoons | 4 tablespoons |
| chicken pieces | 1.5 kg | 3 lb |
| peeled tomatoes | 500 g can | 16 oz can |
| tomato sauce | 250 ml | 1 cup |
| salt | 1 teaspoon | 1 teaspoon |
| pepper | pinch | pinch |
| sugar | 1 teaspoon | 1 teaspoon |
| garlic, crushed | 1-2 cloves | 1-2 cloves |
| celery seeds | ½ teaspoon | ½ teaspoon |
| dried oregano | ½ teaspoon | ½ teaspoon |
| bay leaf (optional) | 1 | 1 |

# equipment

tablespoon measure
teaspoon measure
½ teaspoon measure
cup measure
chopping board

sharp knife
flameproof casserole
tongs or two heatproof spoons
can opener
garlic crusher (optional)

# method

1 Set oven temperature at 170-190°C (350-375°F).

2 Peel and slice onions.

3 Heat oil in a flameproof casserole over a moderate heat.

4 Add chicken pieces a few at a time and brown evenly on all sides (turning them with tongs or two flameproof spoons). Remove from casserole.

5 Add remaining ingredients to casserole, mix well, and heat.

6 Replace chicken pieces in casserole and cover.

7 Cook in a moderate oven for 1½ hours until chicken is tender.

8 Serve with vegetables.

# Cinnamon Squares

SERVES: 4

## ingredients

| | metric | imperial |
|---|---|---|
| bread | 4 slices | 4 slices |
| butter or margarine | 30 g | 1 oz |
| sugar | 2 tablespoons | 2 tablespoons |
| cinnamon | 1 teaspoon | 1 teaspoon |

## equipment

tablespoon measure
teaspoon measure
small saucepan
mixing spoon
knife

# method

1   Pre-heat griller.

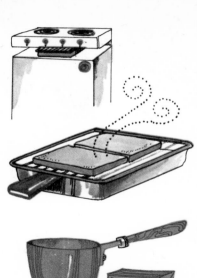

2   Toast one side of each slice of bread under the griller.

3   Melt butter in a small saucepan over a moderate heat.

4   Add sugar and cinnamon and mix well.

5   Spread the mixture evenly over the untoasted side of each slice of bread.

6   Place under the grill until the sugar mixture is crusty and bubbling.

7   Remove from grill, cut off the crusts, and cut into squares.

8   Serve while hot.

# Banana Delight

**SERVES: 2**

# ingredients

| | metric | imperial |
|---|---|---|
| dark block chocolate | 60 g | 2 oz |
| marshmallows | 8 | 8 |
| bananas | 2 | 2 |

# equipment

chopping board
sharp knife
kitchen scissors (optional)
2 pieces of aluminium foil
baking tray

# method

1  Set oven temperature at 200-230°C (375-400°F).

2  Chop chocolate into small pieces.

3  Using kitchen scissors or a sharp knife, halve marshmallows.

4  Peel bananas and cut in half lengthways.

5  Place two banana halves on each piece of aluminium foil.

6  Cover with chopped chocolate and marshmallows.

7  Seal foil packages securely and place on a baking tray.

8  Cook in a moderately hot oven for 15 minutes.

9  Unwrap package carefully: don't burn your fingers!

10  Eat straight from the foil packages.

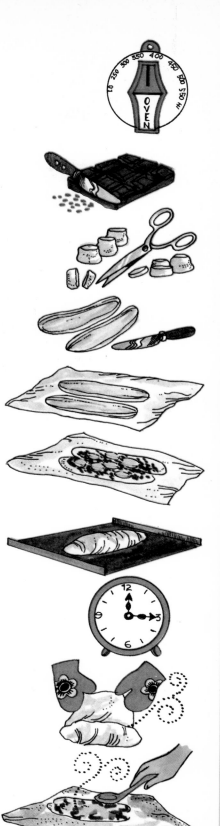

# Pineapple Boat

SERVES: 8-10

## ingredients

| ingredients | metric | imperial |
|---|---|---|
| pineapple | 1 | 1 |
| strawberries | 1 punnet | 1 punnet |
| bananas | 2 | 2 |
| lemon | 1 | 1 |
| sugar | 125 ml | ½ cup |
| passionfruit | 4 | 4 |
| vanilla ice cream | to serve | to serve |

## equipment

cup measure
chopping board
sharp knife
lemon squeezer
large mixing bowl
ice cream scoop or tablespoon

# method

1 Halve pineapple, cutting through leaves and down to base. (The greengrocer may do this for you.)

2 Remove the fruit in slices, without piercing the skin.

3 Discard the hard core and cut fruit into bite-sized pieces.

4 Wash and hull strawberries. Cut them in half if large.

5 Peel and slice bananas.

6 Cut lemon in half and squeeze out juice.

7 In a large mixing bowl, combine pineapple, strawberries, banana, lemon juice and sugar. Mix together thoroughly.

8 Cut passionfruit in half and add pulp to fruit salad.

9 Fill pineapple shells with fruit salad.

10 Serve in bowls with scoops of vanilla ice cream.

# Snowflake Jelly

SERVES: 4

## ingredients

jelly crystals
desiccated coconut
ice cream

## metric and imperial

1 packet
2-3 tablespoons
to serve

## equipment

tablespoon measure
mixing bowl
mixing spoon
jelly mould
serving plate

# method

1 Make up the jelly as directed on the packet.

2 Rinse jelly mould with cold water, then pour jelly into it.

3 Chill in refrigerator until almost set.

4 Stir in coconut and chill in refrigerator until set.

5 Dip the mould into a bowl of hot water for 2-3 seconds. (Do not let water get into jelly in mould.)

6 Cover mould with a serving plate and turn upside-down to remove jelly.

7 Serve with ice cream.

# Pineapple Upside-Down Cake

SERVES: 6-8

# ingredients

| | metric | imperial |
|---|---|---|
| *Topping* | | |
| sliced pineapple | 470 g can | 15 oz can |
| butter or margarine | 60 g | 2 oz |
| brown sugar | 125 ml | ½ cup |
| glacé cherries | 6 | 6 |
| *Cake* | | |
| self-raising flour | 440 ml | 1¾ cups |
| butter or margarine | 95 g | 3 oz |
| sugar | 165 ml | ⅔ cup |
| egg | 1 | 1 |
| milk | 125 ml | ½ cup |

# equipment

cup measure
23 cm (9 inch) cake tin
can opener
small saucepan

wooden spoon
mixing bowl
flour sieve
serving plate

# method

1 Take butter out of refrigerator in advance to soften, and set oven temperature at 170-190°C (350-375°F).

2 Grease a deep, round 23 cm (9 inch) cake tin.

*Topping*
3 Drain pineapple well. Melt butter over a gentle heat and mix with brown sugar.

4 Spread over base of cake tin. Arrange pineapple slices over butter and sugar mixture, placing a cherry in the centre of each slice.
*Cake*
5 Sieve flour.

6 Beat butter and sugar together in a mixing bowl until light and creamy.

7 Add egg and mix in thoroughly.

8 Stir in milk and sieved flour alternately until well blended.

9 Spread cake mixture carefully over pineapple in cake tin and bake in a moderate oven for 45-50 minutes.

10 Remove from oven and allow to stand for 2-3 minutes, then turn upside-down on a serving plate. It is delicious eaten hot or cold, either by itself or with cream or ice cream.

# Crunchy Apple Tart

SERVES: 6-8

# ingredients

| | metric | imperial |
|---|---|---|
| *Pastry* | | |
| plain flour | 375 ml | 1½ cups |
| butter or margarine | 95 g | 3 oz |
| castor sugar | 1 tablespoon | 1 tablespoon |
| egg yolk | 1 | 1 |
| cold water | 1-2 tablespoons | 1-2 tablespoons |
| *Filling and Topping* | | |
| green cooking apples | 3 | 3 |
| butter or margarine | 125 g | 4 oz |
| brown sugar | 125 ml | ½ cup |
| ground cinnamon | 1 tablespoon | 1 tablespoon |
| plain flour | 2 tablespoons | 2 tablespoons |
| walnut pieces | 125 ml | ½ cup |

# equipment

cup measure
tablespoon measure
mixing bowl
flour sieve
mixing spoon
pastry board
rolling pin

23 cm (9 inch) flan ring or pie pla
fork
chopping board
vegetable peeler
sharp knife
small saucepan

# method

1 Set oven temperature at 200-230°C (400-450°F).

*Pastry*

2 Sieve flour into a mixing bowl. Add butter and rub in lightly with fingertips until mixture resembles breadcrumbs.

3 Add sugar and egg yolk, mix well. Then add just enough water to bind dough together.

4 On a floured board, knead dough lightly.

5 Roll pastry out and carefully line a 23 cm (9 inch) flan ring or pie plate.

6 Trim edges with a knife and prick base with a fork to prevent pastry from rising.

*Filling and Topping*

7 Peel, core and slice apples; pack tightly into pastry case.

8 Melt butter over a low heat, add sugar, cinnamon, flour and walnut pieces; mix together.

9 Sprinkle topping over apples and bake tart in a hot oven for 30-35 minutes.

10 Serve hot or cold, by itself or with whipped cream or ice cream.

# Pinapple Fruit Cup

SERVES: 12

# ingredients

| ingredients | metric | imperia |
|---|---|---|
| pineapple juice | 935 ml can | 30 fl oz can |
| apricot nectar | 470 ml can | 15 fl oz can |
| lemonade | 1 litre bottle | 32 fl oz bottle |
| ginger ale | 1 litre bottle | 32 fl oz bottle |
| oranges | 2 | 2 |
| apple | 1 | 1 |
| glacé cherries | 125 g packet | 4 oz packet |
| mint sprigs | to decorate | to decorate |

# equipment

chopping board          large jug
sharp knife             can opener
lemon squeezer          bottle opener
vegetable peeler        tumblers

# method

1  Chill the cans of juice and bottles of drink in advance.

2  Cut the oranges in half and squeeze out the juice.

3  Peel, core and finely chop the apple.

4  Combine all the ingredients in a large jug and mix together thoroughly.

5  Pour fruit cup into tall tumblers and decorate each with a small sprig of mint.